SUMMONED BY BALLS

SUMMONED BY BALLS

BY CHRISTOPHER MATTHEW
DECORATIONS BY DAVID ECCLES

JOHN MURRAY

To Stephen Oliver—
a loyal golfing companion

Text © Christopher Matthew 2005
Illustrations © David Eccles 2005

First published in Great Britain in 2005 by John Murray (Publishers)
A division of Hodder Headline

A CIP catalogue record for this title is available from the British Library

ISBN 0 7195 6819 6

Typeset in Goudy Old Style
by Palimpsest Book Production Limited, Polmont, Stirlingshire

Printed and bound by CPI Bath Press

Hodder Headline policy is to use papers that are natural, renewable and
recyclable products and made from wood grown in sustainable forests. The
logging and manufacturing processes are expected to conform to the
environmental regulations of the country of origin.

John Murray (Publishers)
338 Euston Road
London NW1 3BH

INTRODUCTION

'The least thing upsets him on the links. He misses short putts because of the uproar of the butterflies in the adjoining meadows.'

Of the myriad wits and sages who have pronounced on the game of golf over the years, none has hit the proverbial on the head more neatly and more often than the great P.G. Wodehouse. An enthusiastic golfer of modest achievements, who was convinced that any hole under 500 yards was reachable in one shot, he realised early on that golf is a metaphor for life. No one, golfer or non-golfer, dare take anything for granted – least of all when things are going like a breeze.

'Golf acts as a corrective against sinful pride,' Wodehouse wrote in a story entitled 'The Magic Plus-Fours'. 'I attribute the insane arrogance of the later Roman emperors almost entirely to the fact that, never having played golf, they never knew that strange, chastening humility which is engendered by a topped chip-shot. If Cleopatra had been ousted in the first round of the Ladies' Singles, we should have heard a lot less of her proud imperiousness.'

But no matter how much players may grouse about their persistent slice and their appalling score in the monthly medal, golf brings infinitely more joy than pain. Not only is it played in some of the most beautiful surroundings in the world, but few other games lay quite such store by sportsmanship, honesty, generosity of spirit and good manners. Golfers always praise their opponents' good shots and commiserate on their bad ones. At the conclusion of every round, players doff their caps and shake hands before leaving the green. In the bar, disappointments melt away in the general atmosphere of bonhomie. Golf has spawned some of the most crashing bores of all time, but more often than not one finds oneself in the company of the best humoured, most exuberant and most entertaining people one could possibly wish to meet.

Indeed, disaster – or the prospect of it – often engenders the funniest and most memorable moments. One of the worst afflictions with which any golfer can be laid low, be it in the US Masters or during a Saturday afternoon pick-up foursome, is the sudden and total inability to putt – known as the 'yips'. Alistair Cooke and the great golf writer, Henry Longhurst, were once on their way to the first tee when Cooke enquired, 'Have you ever had the yips, Henry?' Longhurst replied, 'Actually, no.' He paused for a moment, then added, 'But I'm afraid I may be a carrier.'

This book celebrates the wide variety of characters, the highs and the lows, the tragedies and the triumphs that are the warp and woof of one of the most infuriating, compulsive and altogether enjoyable forms of activity ever invented.

CONTENTS

FIRST TEE
(*after* THE EAGLE by Alfred, Lord Tennyson)

He grasps the club and bends his arms,
He twists his neck and wets his palms,
While softly whistling bits of Brahms.

He summons up his natural class,
Adjusts his ball, adjusts his arse—
And drives straight into knee-high grass.

AMATEUR
(*after* YOUNG EXECUTIVE by John Betjeman)

I am a real amateur. No clubs than mine are older;
I have an ancient golf bag, with a half-torn golf-
  ball holder.
My putter's shaft is hickory, my woods are real wood;
I'd change them if I thought that it would do me
  any good.

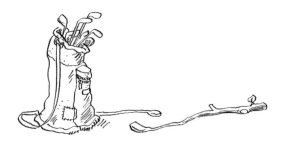

I wear a pair of corduroys in every kind of weather,
A cardigan and pork-pie hat the colour of dead
  heather.
My golf shoes have seen better days; they're
  missing half their studs.
My balls are mostly pick-ups, so they're also mostly
  duds.

I've got a smelly Labrador. I call him Old Plum Duff.
He can't keep up for toffee, but he's brilliant in the
   rough.
While others slash through thorns and gorse and
   curse their wayward shots,
He finds my ball in seconds in the most unlikely
   spots.

You ask me what's my handicap. To be completely
  frank,
I'm not exactly what you'd call a chap in the top
  rank.
Officially it's 21, but seriously, mate,
The way I'm playing nowadays, it's nearer 28.

My name has never featured on a cup or silver
  plate.
In club games I am never asked if I could add my
  weight.
I haven't done a medal round for over forty
  years—
I'm not at all competitive like many of my peers.

I look at my contemporaries with all their fancy
  gear—
Their great big shiny drivers which they change
  from year to year.
And when I hear them banging on about their
  latest scores,
I give three cheers for amateurs: thank God, we're
  never bores!

THE EXPERT
(*after* LOCHINVAR by Sir Walter Scott)

Oh, Oliver Grout has sat down in his vest;
As golf experts go, he could pass any test.
With a beer by his side and a fag in his hand,
There is no shrewder judge in the whole of the
    land.
He's the fount of all wisdom, week in and week
    out—
He's the new Peter Alliss, is Oliver Grout.

He rarely has lunch or nips out for a pee
When one of the Opens is on the TV.
He daren't miss a drive, or a putt, or a chip
Of the Masters or PGA Championship;
And delivers a stream of statistics throughout—
For a storehouse of knowledge, is Oliver Grout.

He could walk the first round in a *Mastermind* quiz
With quick-fire replies to obscure questions—viz:
What was John Daly's score in the Buick last year?
Whose caddy at Lytham deserved a thick ear?
Which golfer's great passion is fishing for trout?
There'd be no silly 'passes' for Oliver Grout.

His technical know-how is second to none—
He could give a few tips to the world Number One.
He knows his way round every championship course,
And can pinpoint, at Troon, every last inch of
    gorse.
But strangest of all—there's no shadow of doubt—
He has never played golf in his life, Ollie Grout.

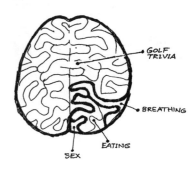

SECOND THOUGHTS
(*after* SIR PATRICK SPENS. Anon.)

Gervaise strode off the seventeenth green
And cursed like Attila the Hun—
'Oh how could I have been three holes up
And lose by two and one?'

Gervaise was not a man for words
When he had lost his rag;
He threw his putter in a bush,
And then he grabbed his bag.

He marched across the clubhouse lawn—
'It's more than I can take!'
He hoisted up his bag of clubs
And threw it in the lake.

This ghastly deed was watched with awe
By members in the bar.
He gave them all a victory sign
And went to fetch his car.

The sky grew dark, the clouds rolled in,
A chilly north wind blew;
Then, as the members shook their heads,
Gervaise hove into view.

He marched across the lawn again
And straight into the mere.
He seized the bag and raised it high
And heard the members cheer.

He carried it as lovingly
As Tarzan carried Jane,
Undid the zip, took out his keys,
And threw it back again.

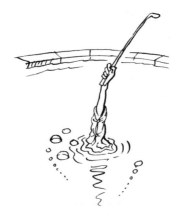

WILDLIFE
(*after* CARGOES by John Masefield)

Half-blind Labrador from north-west Norfolk,
Plodding up the seventh on a steamy June day,
With a tongue like a dishcloth,
Bumping into bunkers,
Wishing he was not the only one too old to play.

Perky Border Terrier in darkest Ayrshire,
Tearing through the heather like a small Force 4,
With a grin like a lunatic,
Digging up the fairway,
Snapping here and crapping there and being a
    bore.

Cocky Cocker Spaniel with a nose like a truffle-
   hound,
Dashing round the bushes in his own mad game,
With a prize of two thousand
Top Flites, Titleists,
Slazengers, Callaways and lifelong fame.

CLUB GRUB
(*after* MY FAVOURITE THINGS
by Oscar Hammerstein)

Mulligatawny and egg mayonnaises,
Plum tart with custard and chocolate daisies,
Old-fashioned, no-nonsense, good English grub—
This is my favourite food at the club.

Bangers and mash served with lashings of gravy,
Thick treacle tart like they cooked in the navy,
Cheeses you find in a good country pub—
This is my favourite food at the club.

Sirloin of beef piled with parsnip and carrot,
Washed down with oodles of plain, honest claret,
Horseradish sauce that's so strong that you blub—
This is my favourite food at the club.

When the wind howls,
When my swing goes,
When I'm feeling flat,
If I can't cheer up with a lunch and a doze,
Then, dammit, I'll eat . . . my hat!

WIFE DESCENDING
(*after* THE DESTRUCTION OF
SENNACHERIB by Lord Byron)

Mrs Hotchkiss came down like a half-ton of bricks,
And her face was as dark as the dead on the Styx,
And her hair was as clenched as a golf-player's fist
When his pitiful partner has putted and missed.

Like hailstones in June on the seventeenth green
In the worst summer storm that has ever been
   seen;
Like the Pro-Hunt Alliance in Parliament Square,
There was no one who wasn't aware she was there.

The face of her husband turned white as a loon,
And his eyeballs popped out like a Bateman
  cartoon—
THE MAN WHO SAID 'OKAY THEN, ONE FOR
  THE ROAD',
Now suddenly looked like a well-harrowed toad,

While his cronies all sat there as if they'd been
  shot,
Their bodies as stiff as the poor wife of Lot,
And the air in the bar turned a delicate blue
In the subsequent, blood-chilling hullabaloo.

To this day there's a crack in the Smoking Room
    wall,
And the woodwork is scorched round the door in
    the hall.
It warns those who break the unbreakable code,
And dare to say, 'Okay then, one for the road.'

OVERDOING IT
(after LIFE by Dorothy Parker)

Oh golf's one long round of pure pleasure and
    fun—
A feast of profound satisfaction.
I bet twenty quid I could outdrive my son,
Now I'm spending a fortnight in traction.

HOWEVER
(*after* IF by Rudyard Kipling)

However many hours I try to practise,
And tinker with my multi-tinkered swing,
And steel myself to drive off from the back tees
And, having done so, think myself a king.
However many times I change equipment,
From Callaway to Ping and TaylorMade,
And know how much my artificial hip meant,
And tell myself I'm lucky to have played.
However many times I make up numbers
In pick-up rounds on Saturdays at two,
And tread the floor in lion-hearted rhumbas
With captains' wives—and sometimes captains, too.

Though fragile as a Pawnee's broken arrow,
I've never once looked less than in the pink;
And even when I'm poorer than a sparrow,
I'm always first to say, 'My shout, I think!'
However many times I lose to losers,
Yet never make a face to show I care,
And laugh at silly comments made by boozers,
Or racist jibes, and never turn a hair.
However hard I work at being witty,
And setting all the ladies on a roar,

And badgering the Handicap Committee
With cards that prove I'm less than 24.
However many years I've been a member,
And done my bit and played a member's part,
And shown my face from April to December,
And given all—my life, my soul, my heart.
Yet still I count for little in this set-up;
The barman never seems to know my name.
I spend my waking hours getting het up,
And—what is more—I'm useless at the game.

LADY GOLFER
(*after* LENTEN THOUGHTS OF A HIGH ANGLICAN by John Betjeman)

Isn't she gorgeous, the Golfer?
With her smoothly tanned, long, long legs,
And the flash of her waist every time that she swings,
Or bends down to pick up her pegs?

How nonchalantly she takes the club,
How lazy her follow-through!
Sad men rediscover the love of their youth,
And mentally scrawl billets-doux.

But she never sees the sly glances
They steal as she heads for the first,
For she is the new ladies' champion,
And a five-handicapper at worst.

She triumphs in mixed competitions,
And sets an unbeatable pace,
As men find they lose concentration—
Not to mention the grin from their face.

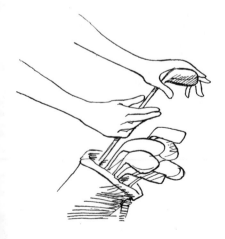

But few ever mind being beaten
By a woman they'd all love to date;
For an hour or two in her presence
Is enough to make all men feel great.

THE MODERN PRO
(*after* THE MAJOR-GENERAL'S SONG in
THE PIRATES OF PENZANCE
by W.S. Gilbert)

I am the very pattern of a modern tour
professional;
At tournaments I treat each interview as a
confessional.
I analyse each shot I've played in language quite
fanatical—
'I'm hitting pretty solid' is my notion of
grammatical.
The agonies I go through on the course are
psychological;
My marital arrangements, though, are nigh on
mythological.
My caddy Ron and I are known as golfing's Dave
and Jonathan;
There's no one I would rather have alongside
when I'm on a run.
My coach devotes his waking life to changing my
parabola
With talk of geometric planes and ultimate
hyperbola.
I sometimes think my whole career is one long,
slow recessional:
I am the very model of a modern golf professional.

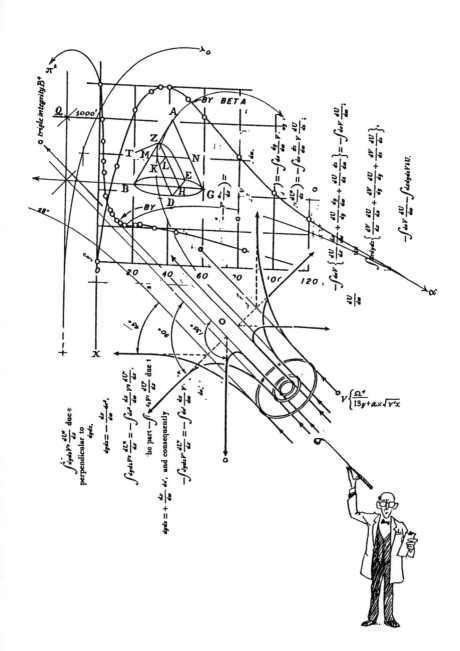

HEAVEN

(*after* A SUBALTERN'S LOVE-SONG
by John Betjeman)

Oh West Hunterdown! Oh West Hunterdown!
A golf club to die for, an hour from town.
What rounds I have played there with Adam, and
     Nick,
And Charlie, and Charlie's wife's ex-husband, Dick!

No fairways are greener, no greens are more lush—
The woods echo softly with blackbird and thrush.
The azaleas glow like a bridal bouquet,
And even the heather is lovely in May.

On guest days in summer the buffet is fab—
The sideboards are piled high with lobster and crab.
Proceedings kick off with a generous snort,
Then the wine flows like water and, after that, port.

The afternoon games are invariably rounds
Full of squiffy-eyed air-shots and balls out of bounds,
And the crack and the rattle of firmly struck trees,
With the prospect of strawbugs and crumbly cream
     teas.

The locker room crackles with civilised wit,
And everyone there thinks that Blair is a twit,
And makes jokes about Blunkett and Brown and
     the Dome—
Nowhere else have I ever felt quite so at home.

The membership list reads like Evelyn Waugh,
With hyphens and knighthoods and titles and
    more.
How I long to be one of this rollicking bunch,
With my name on my locker, and friends down for
    lunch.

I know lots of members who say it's a crime
That my name's not come up—it's a matter of
    time.
I've been in the book now for three years at least;
Must I wait in fond hope till a member's deceased?

I've had drinks with the captain—the president,
  too.
And I've mentioned my problem to goodness
  knows who.
But hard though I try, both down there and in
  town,
I'm still not a member of West Hunterdown.

PAST IT
(*after* THE RIME OF THE ANCIENT
MARINER by Samuel Taylor Coleridge)

Al was an old-age pensioner,
Who retired at sixty-three,
With slightly raised cholesterol
And a slightly dodgy knee.

While others jogged and took long walks,
He never once broke sweat.
His ideal milieu remained
The cocktail-party set.

His doctor said, 'You're getting fat,
And while you've still got vim,
You ought to take some exercise,
And work out in the gym.'

Al told a chum in Basingstoke,
Who said, 'He must be mad—
Golf is the game for chaps our age.
Just take my word, old lad.'

He thrilled him with his fighting words—
Al stood there all agog.
'The game's about as arduous
As falling off a log . . .'

         *   *   *

Now Al's an old-age pensioner
With whisky on his breath.
With trembling hands and staring eyes
He bores his friends to death.

He holds them in an iron grip—
'There is a game,' says he,
'That haunts men morning, night and noon,
From which they can't break free.

'I bought the clubs, I bought the kit,
I signed up with a pro.
For three long months I tried to hit
A ball and make it go.

'Week after week, month after month,
I tried without progressing—
An ill-coordinated lump,
Increasingly depressing.

'Golfers, golfers everywhere
In colours bright and gay;
Golfers, golfers everywhere,
Yet all I saw was grey.

'My very soul did weep! Dear God!
How could I be so bad?
How could a game be less fun than
The siege of Leningrad?

'Alone, alone, all, all alone,
I suffered pangs of hell.
I could not sleep, I could not eat,
My hair fell out as well.

'Don't ever take up golf, old lad,'
He says to all who'll hear.
'But, if you must, don't wait until
You're stiff and old and sere.'

No matter what your temperament,
Serene or highly strung—
Golf's like a nasty dose of mumps,
It should be caught when young.

CLUBMAN
(*after* THE COW by Robert Louis Stevenson)

My pal Ken Hall from Donegal
Is pissed from noon till night.
He's five foot wide and six foot tall—
A plus-foured sybarite.

His hair is white, his face bright red,
His eyes are soft, and gleam
Like two poached eggs upon a bed
Of strawberries and cream.

He tacks his way from tee to green
(Though mostly in the rough):
A multi-coloured brigantine
That's running low on puff.

And in the bar from twelve till two
He holds the place agog
With tales of golfing derring-do
In seamless monologue.

WIDOWS
(*after* BUSINESS GIRLS by John Betjeman)

Soothing sounds of daytime telly,
Ticking clocks and hourly chimes
Haunt ten thousand golfing widows
Thumbling through their *Radio Times*.

Everything is done and dusted,
Dinner wrapped in cellophane,
Dishcloths washed and flowery cushions
Plumped up on the counterpane.

'Sure you'll be okay, then, darling?'
Why they bother no one knows.
'I could cancel if you'd rather.'
I *could* punch you on the nose.

Novels by Joanna Trollope,
Bubble baths at half past three,
Gins and tonics sipped, abandoned,
Cupsa soup and mugsa tea.

Phone calls halfway through *EastEnders*:
'Be bit late, love; don't wait dins.'
Cheese on toast and woolly slippers,
Unwrapped dinners dumped in bins.

SPECTATORS
(*after* TARANTELLA by Hilaire Belloc)

Did you remember the gin,
Amanda?
Did you remember the gin?
And the tonic and the Players,
And the woollies and the layers,
And the hats for the gnats
That look better on prats,
And the Ambre Solaire No. 2,
And the kir and the beer just in case we feel
    queer?
(Puts me in mind of that day in Uganda.)

Do you remember King's Lynn, Amanda?
Do you remember King's Lynn?
When they danced the beguine by the seventeenth
    green,
And the crowd went bananas,
Like mad Lippizaners,
And the secretary played the tambourine?
And the corks went pop
On the top
Of the greenkeeper's hut for the putt
By a chap called Trumping—
Bumping,
Jumping,
Bouncing and thumping
Smack in the back of the cup.
And the crowd went up
With the eeks and the shrieks and hurrahs?

Did you remember the gin,
Amanda?
Did you remember the gin?
And the ice,
Amanda?
And a slice
Of lemon would be nice,
And some peanuts we could nibble once or twice.
Some chocs
In a box, and a spare pair of socks.
A jug
For the Pimms, and a rug, and binocs,
And stocks
Of champagne,
So we'll laugh and we'll dance in the rain.

CLERIHEWS

Colin Montgomerie
Has suffered a lifetime of flummery.
Whether he'd win a major
Was something no one would wager.

Ernie is called the Big Easy
'Cos he makes golf look easy-peasy.
He must sometimes chortle
That he's not like the average mortal.

EXCUSES, EXCUSES
(*after* THE LADY IS A TRAMP
by Lorenz Hart)

I haven't picked up a club since last week.
I've got this blister and walk like a freak.
I tweaked my neck and my swing's up the creek.
That's why I'm playing like a drain.

I've got new glasses and can't see a thing.
I can't get used to this putter by Ping.
I keep expecting my builder to ring.
That's why I'm playing like a drain.

I like a warm, dry morning in May,
Smell of new hay,
Nice job, no prob.
This wind is proving one hell of a strain.
That's why I'm playing like a drain.

I had a row with my girlfriend last night.
I can't decide if she's really Miss Right.
And now she's gone to the Isle of Wight.
That's why I'm playing like a drain.

I like a few quiet holes with some chums,
No noisy bums.
One joke, I choke.
I don't believe it! Do I hear a train?
Oh God, I'm playing like a drain.

It's not my fault that a dog grabbed my ball,
Or that that tree on the sixth was so tall,
Or that the holes on this course are too small.
I can't help playing like a drain.

When I was sitting at home watching pros,
I thought I could be the new Justin Rose,
But I got stung by a bee up my nose.
That's why I'm playing like a drain.

I like to play the way that I please,
Go like a breeze—
Hush hush, no rush.
Would you believe it! It's starting to rain,
And I'm still playing like a drain.

WINNING WAYS
(*after* THE KISS by Coventry Patmore)

'I swear I saw them cheat.' 'You sure?'
'I'm sure I'm sure.' 'The little rats!'
'They think a win is now secure.'
'They think we think they think we're prats.'

KEVIN BLING
(*after* CAUTIONARY TALES by Hilaire Belloc)

The chief defect of Kevin Bling
Was, basically . . . well . . . everything.
His hand and eye were not as one,
His golf was, frankly, hit-and-run.
The balls flew off just anyhow—
One even struck a passing cow.
Another hit a nearby oak;
The ball fell out, and then a bloke,
Who sat there, both hands on his head.
'Winged him!' was all young Kevin said.

One day he drove across the road
And hit a giant lorryload
Of turnips and assorted veg.
The driver swerved right through a hedge,
And hit a row of deckchairs—twice.
Bling said, 'That's nice. That's *very* nice.'
Those in the know would flock to see
His exploits on the opening tee.

Once, after lunch, he clipped the ball
Smartly into the clubhouse hall.
It rapped a picture on the right,
Flew up and smashed the electric light,
Bounced off a hideous piece of brass,
And struck the barman on the arse.
The pro devoted countless hours
And all his best professional powers
To changing Kevin's dreadful swing—
His stance, his grip, his everything,
But finally confessed defeat.
He said, 'This one has got me beat.

Whatever new technique I try,
I might as well teach pigs to fly.'
Now Kevin's put away his clubs
And spends his time in local pubs,
And empties bars and chills men's hearts
With four short words: 'Right. Who's for darts?'

BUSINESS IN HAND
(*after* VITAÏ LAMPADA by Sir Henry Newbolt)

There's a breathless hush—it is close, all right—
Two holes up and just three to go;
A splitting head and a fading light,
And the client's round is a tale of woe.
I'm ahead despite several short putts missed,
And wayward drives and lunchtime booze,
And my boss's warning, gently hissed,
'Remember, chum, you're here to schmooze.'

These are the words that once a year
Summon young men like a witch's curse.
We play like dogs, but still we fear
Our clients will play even worse.
We do our very best to fail,
And, as the last putt drops, we muse
Upon our fate, and rage and rail,
'To hell with golf, and booze, and schmooze!'

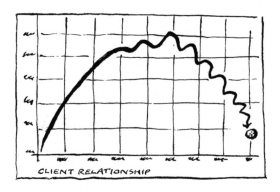

CLIENT RELATIONSHIP

TALKING BALLS
(after AFTER BLENHEIM *by Robert Southey)*

It was a summer evening,
　　The daily race was run,
And Betty's feet were on the pouffe—
　　The News had just begun,
When through the door with bag on back
Came red-faced, golf-mad husband, Jack.

He dropped the bag, he puffed and groaned
　　As is the golfer's way;
Yet seemed, once settled in his chair,
　　Unusually gay.
She concentrated on the screen,
Maintaining an indifferent mien.

Jack gave a modest cough and said,
　　'I'm never one to boast,
But on the fifteenth green today,
　　The man I played was toast.
In fact I beat him 4 & 3—
A good result, you must agree.

'I wouldn't want to bore you, love
    With every shot I played;
Suffice to say my chips and putts
    Put all his in the shade.
My wedge shot to the second green
Was better than I've ever seen.'

'I've had a busy day myself,'
    Said Betty with a yawn.
'I plumbed the sink and wormed the cat,
    And then I mowed the lawn.
I cleaned the house from top to toe;
Since first thing I've been on the go.'

Jack ummed and urred and sucked his teeth,
    And gently rubbed one ear,
And, jumping to his feet, he said,
    'I wouldn't mind a beer.
My mouth is like a parrot's cage;
Right now I'm feeling twice my age.

'I had some trouble on the eighth,
    And also on the tenth.
My drive had got a lovely shape,
    But hadn't got the length.
The green was further than it looked.
"My God," I thought. "That's it. I'm cooked!"

'But, blow me down, he topped his chip,
    So I took out my 6,
And, as I swung, thought, "Now's the time
    To show my box of tricks."
I put it two feet from the pin,
It stopped, spun back and dribbled in.'

'I'm off to pack now,' Betty said,
    'I shan't be very long.
But please don't let me interrupt,
    And please don't get me wrong.
Your glorious tales of cut and thrust
From here on in I'll take on trust.'

Jack stood beside the old front door
   And waved a fond goodbye,
And shook his head and blew his nose,
   And sighed a little sigh.
'How odd. For after all,' said he,
'It was a cracking victory.'

LIMERICK

A handsome young golfer called Norm
Got caught in a wild thunderstorm.
In a moment of folly
He put up his brolly,
And now looks like Somerset Maugham.

CLOCK GOLF
(*after* HOW THEY BROUGHT THE GOOD
NEWS FROM AIX TO GHENT
by Robert Browning)

We leapt in the Volvo, old Boris and me;
We had to abandon our last cup of tea.
'Good luck!' cried my wife as we shot through the
   gate.
'We'll need it,' I muttered. 'We're half an hour
   late.'
The lights turned to red at the end of our street;
So did I. Boris smiled and said, 'Isn't life sweet?'

We crawled on in silence down Kentish Town Road
At the speed of an elderly, arthritic toad.
Our tee-off was scheduled for 9.42—
By 8 we were just about passing the Zoo.
Boris said that he knew a quick way through Hyde
    Park—
I thought to myself, 'Well, blow that for a lark.'

We reached Fulham Broadway at twenty to nine;
Boris said, 'Keep this up and I'm sure we'll be
    fine.'
The traffic in Putney was all nose-to-tail;
Boris said, 'Trust me, lad, we'll get there without fail.
Take a left at the lights and dodge up round the
    back—
When it comes to south London, I've got quite a
    knack.'

We turned left and then right and went on for a
    bit
Over sleeping policemen, then suddenly hit
Some damned one-way system: before we knew
    what,
We were back where we started and losing the plot.
It was just after 9 when we met the A3—
'Put your foot down,' said Boris, as calm as could
    be.

'Hold your horses!' I cried. 'There are cameras
    about!
Keep your eyes skinned and, if you should see one,
    please shout.'
We cruised past Roehampton at 40 or less—
By Robin Hood Way, I was feeling the stress.
'Stop fussing,' said Boris, 'and don't be a berk;
They are put there to warn us. They none of them
    work.'

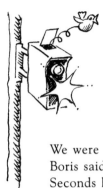

We were flashed at Raynes Park doing 71—
Boris said, 'Just forget it. They do that for fun.'
Seconds later we ground to a halt in a jam.
I was frankly in need of a cardiogram.
Boris hummed and he hahed: 'We'll be here for a
    week.
I suggest that we plump for the *route touristique*.'

We shot through East Molesey, and West Molesey,
    too,
And from Walton to Shepperton onward we flew.
The sun on the river gleamed bright by our side—
'I told you we'd make it on time,' Boris cried.
We stopped off in Weybridge to have a quick pee,
And were clamped by a warden at 9.33.

Boris said, 'It's a bore, but then what can you do?
Let's count all our blessings and take a broad view.
Here we are in the sunshine, the birds in the trees
Are chirping their heads off, and life is a breeze.
So what if our names don't appear on the board?
We're alive, and at our age that's ample reward.

'Golf's a game, chum, let's face it—no more and
  no less;
We can play when we like, we're not under duress.'
So we found a nice pub and we drank lots of beer,
And we told silly jokes and were full of good
  cheer.
Then we drove back to town feeling fifteen feet
  tall,
And the subject of golf wasn't mentioned at all.

TO AN EX-LADY CAPTAIN
(*after* TO A FAT LADY SEEN FROM A TRAIN by Frances Cornford)

O why do you dress like a whipped-cream meringue,
    Crossed with a fully rigged yacht?
O dreaded purveyor of *Sturm und* of *Drang*,
Why do you dress like a whipped-cream meringue,
With that face like a dyspeptic orang-utang,
    And the nose of a mad guillemot?
And why must you talk in a non-stop harangue—
    Most of it absolute rot?

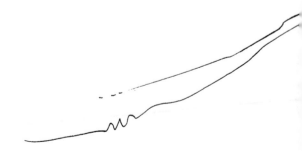

FUN
(*after* LEISURE by W.H. Davies)

What is this game if, full of grief,
We have no time for light relief?

No time to pause and watch a flight
Of geese across the fading light,

Or miss a drive by half a yard,
And say, 'This course is much too hard!'

Or muff a two-foot putt, or less,
And punch the air, and shout out 'Yes!'

No time to pull the captain's leg,
And throw the odd symbolic egg,

Or squeeze the lady captain's thigh
And murmur, 'Well, it's worth a try . . .'

Or wear a bog-roll tie to lunch
And call the steward 'Honeybunch',

And spout a load of drunken blah,
And dance the cancan on the bar,

And when invited to resign,
Say, 'Good idea! Next round is mine!'

Yet, what's the point of light relief
If all it brings is pain and grief?

MIXED BLESSINGS
(*after* HUNTER TRIALS by John Betjeman)

It's jolly bad luck on Lysander;
    His dad made a mess of the last.
Now he's sulking out on the verandah—
    His chances of winning are past.

I wish I could say that I'm sorry;
    Lysander's my best friend at school.
He's Captain of Games at The Quarry,
    But his father's an absolute fool.

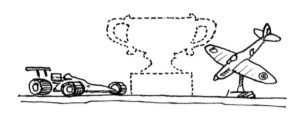

I *do* want to be this year's winner
  Of the Fathers' and Sons' Under-12,
And to take the cup back home to Pinner—
  There's a space on the dining-room shelf.

The Dalrymples were leading all morning,
  The McBains couldn't keep up for nuts,
When, without any reason or warning,
  Harry's dad missed a couple of putts.

Then he started to play like a clunker;
  Every shot was a slice or a shank.
He took three to get out of one bunker,
  And his chipping and putting were rank.

The Robertsons beat the O'Briens,
    Which nobody thought that they could,
But Tom made a muck of his irons,
    And his dad made a muck of his wood.

Mrs Johnson's as sick as a parrot—
    She was certain that Daniel would win,
But her husband drank far too much claret,
    And was pretty much out of his skin.

It's not easy to play with your father—
  I know mine would rather be dead.
To be honest I'd really much rather
  Play with somebody else's instead.

Which is why I am playing with Tristan's—
  He's won this event twice before.
I'm sure that he won't have got pissed and
  We're sure to record a good score.

*   *   *

We played like a pair made in heaven;
  We were two up with just two to play,
When he hit his own foot with a 7—
  That's the end of our golf for today.

HAIKUS

Empire of the Sun—
Millions swing on rubber mats,
And say they played well.

Golfers on ranges
Win about as often as
Archers without arrows.

SCOTCH MIST

(*after* HIAWATHA by Henry Longfellow—with
apologies to Robert Burns)

By the ninth at Trimbly Bottom,
Near the sands of Hell's Bells Bunker,
Stood the shop of Old McHaggis,
Son of mighty Jack McHaggis.
Right beside it, in the car park,
Stood the Mercs and shiny Volvos,
Telling of the wealth of members.

Way beyond it stretched the fairway,
Stretched the green and wicked fairway,
Stretched the tenth at Trimbly Bottom.
There the wrinkled old McHaggis
Taught the keen young Alexander—
Took a cut-down 7 iron,
Silver-shafted, leather-handled,
Polished bright with kitchen wire wool.
Taught him how to swing it slowly,
Smooth as Islay's best malt whisky,
Murmuring soft words of wisdom:
'Gang ye weel, ye bonnie laddie,
Gang a-gley, my lee-lang fiere.
Wa' wi' ye wi' bickering brattle,
Gie's a hand, ye sleekit beastie,
Blessings on your sleety dribble.

We weel rin aba' the brae-side,
Tak' na' heed for auld acquaintance.
Willie waught tak' twa' thegither,
Scots wa'hey for houghmagandie!
May your tass for aye hang low.'

LOCAL KNOWLEDGE
(*after* THE HORSE. Anon.)

I know two things about this course,
And one of them is bloody gorse.

SO, FAREWELL . . .
(*after* THE BURIAL OF SIR JOHN MOORE AT CORUNNA by Charles Wolfe)

Not an eye is sad, not a tear is shed,
    As the balls up the eighteenth we carry;
Not one member complains, or shakes his head
    As we say our farewells to old Harry.

The wind from the north brings a glow to our
                                                  cheeks
  As we stand round the tee in a huddle,
And the captain pulls on his nose as he speaks
  Of our friend, Monsieur Harry Tolpuddle.

He recounts some old tales of the days of his
                                                  prime,
  When he'd roll up and play in pyjamas;
And remembers when Harry and Montagu Syme
  Were ordered to leave the Bahamas.

Then we all add our own little snapshot or scene
  Of a memorable Tolpuddle caper—
Like the classic performance of 'God Save the Queen',
  With Harry on bug-rake and paper.

When the moment arrives for the final adieu,
    We all take a ball and a driver,
And as each of us hits, we shout out 'Toodle-oo!'
    To this reprobate joker and skiver.

As each ball rockets skyward above the deep
                                   rough,
    Like a soul on a paradise stairway,
It explodes with a pop and dissolves in a puff,
    Which floats on past the seventeenth fairway.

Though the mortal remains of that once handsome
frame
Are now sprinkled half over north Devon,
Yet his spirit will live just as long as the game
In the spot that for Harry was Heaven.

DRIVE IT LIKE TIGER
(*after* THE WAY THROUGH THE WOODS
by Rudyard Kipling)

They closed the membership list
Two or three years ago.
The old boys who play quite like it that way,
And now no amount of dough
Can get your name on the list.
You may be gifted and keen,
With a dream of a swing and a talent to match,
But you're just not on the scene.
And it does seem frightfully mean
That people are prejudiced,
And an unknown of nineteen
Can never get on to the list.

But one will dare to persist;
And on a summer's eve,
When the sun is low and the breezes blow
And the last few members leave,
And the ones in the bar are pissed—
As the grass grows damp with dew,
He'll play a round with a chap from the town,
And the word will filter through
That suddenly, out of the blue,
There's a talent that daren't be missed;
And it's time that someone new
Was put on the membership list . . .
Though there is no membership list.

SINGLETON
(*after* WAITING AT THE WINDOW
by A.A. Milne)

I'm standing on the eighteenth tee
On Wednesday afternoon at three.

I've had some pars—a birdie, too;
I'd like a score of 92.

I'm playing with my Top Flite 4;
It's done me very well before.

I hit my driver really well
To find I've played the shot from hell.

I caught the damned thing off the toe;
No wonder it went really low.

I thought that I was being deft—
I've hit a hazard on the left.

If I could catch it nice and clean
I'd land it somewhere near the green.

Oh, bollocks! Now look what I've done!
I've topped it; it'll never run.

Oh God, it's plugged against a bank.
I hit it much too hard—and shank!

Oh, this is quite beyond a joke;
I'd best drop out and lose a stroke.

I'll hit a wedge. I'm in a fix!
No! On the green, for only six!

I judge the borrow; line it up.
It's going in . . . it's in the cup!

Hurray! I've ended up all square!
Golf's better on one's own, I swear.

And better still, safe in the womb
Of warmth and comfort in one's room.

TREASURES IN THE ATTIC
(*after* LITTLE BOY BLUE by Eugene Field)

The hickory driver is covered with dust,
    The polish is faded and scratched,
And the trusty old niblicks are red with rust,
    And the head of the spoon's detached.
Time was when those clubs were the best you
                                could buy,
    And the twine round the brassie was tight;
But that was a time long ago when the sky,
    Like the future, was rosy and bright.

'Your father was one of the best,' they said.
  For a decade he played off two.
He won cup after cup and consistently led
  In medals and matchplay, too.
He would drive long and low and incredibly straight,
  But, if needed, could bend it round trees.
He dropped thirty-foot putts at a breathtaking rate,
  And chipped with phenomenal ease.

But no one has taken his clubs out to play
    For sixty years or more.
The red leather grips have crumbled away
    In the dust on the attic floor.
And few men at the club can now recall
    Dad's name, as men did before,
But it's there on the board on the clubroom wall—
    'To the Dead of the Second World War.'

OUT OF THIS WORLD
(*after* WHEN YOU WISH UPON A STAR
by Ned Washington)

When you swing among the stars,
On the Moon or out on Mars,
Levity will guarantee
The sun shines through.

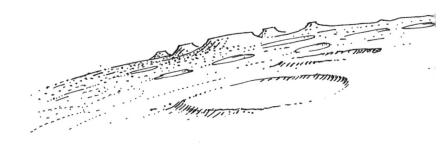

THE CALL OF THE WILD
(*after* SEA FEVER by John Masefield)

I must nip off for a pee again; if I don't, I may
    well die.
And all I ask is a small bush about four or five
    feet high,
And a clear view and a quick slash and a
    moment's shaking,
And a light wind and a good zip that's not forever
    breaking.

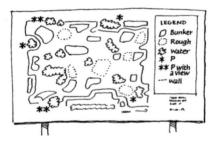

I must pop off for a pee again, Dame Nature won't
    be denied;
And there's nothing more fun than a pee in the
    sun, as anyone knows who's tried.
And the breeze through the trees brings a sense of
    ease, with the white clouds scudding,
And the gulls' cry in the blue sky, and the wild
    flowers budding . . .

I must take care where I pee again; I'd have sworn
  there was no one near.
There wasn't a soul for miles around, just some
  crows and a distant deer.
And I had to choose the only place on the whole
  of the ruddy course
Where the vicar was down on his hands and
  knees, hunting for balls in the gorse.

RESIGNATION
(*after* THE LAST LAUGH by John Betjeman)

I played golf on the Algarve.
   My back went.
Though my best days are over
   And my swing spent,
There's always golf on the telly
   In north-east Kent.